LIVING A LIFE OF ABUNDANCE

THE 67 AIKIDO PRINCIPLES TO GROW WEALTH, JOY AND TOTAL FREEDOM!

360° Lifestyle Series No.1
The easy, simple and practical way to choose,
create and grow a joyful life

Health and Wealth Warning!
Satisfactory Result or Money-back Guarantee!

Please read this warning before you start reading this booklet. It contains powerful secrets and timeless precepts that are capable of transforming and changing your life beyond your dreams and expectations. The secrets are only for the brave, the bold and the courageous ones ready to change their lives. Well, you have been warned and if it is to be, it is up to you. This book is sold with one-year-money-back guarantee or warrantee. The contents have worked for many people and the author guarantees that they would work for you. But if for any reason you are not absolutely satisfied with the results of applying the principles, simply send it back with receipt to your vendor for a full refund. And when they work for you, please pass it on to others and do us a favour by letting us know!

LIVING A LIFE
OF ABUNDANCE

BOLA DAUDA

ROBIN BOOKS · LIVERPOOL

© Bola Dauda 2006
First published in Great Britain 2006

PB ISBN 1-904843-12-3
HB ISBN 1-904843-13-1

Published by
Robin Books Limited
110 Tower Street, Brunswick Business Park,
Century Building, Liverpool L3 4BJ.

Additional copies of this book can be ordered from:
Website: www.robinbooks.co.uk
E-mail: readers@robinbooks.co.uk
or
Freepost: RLXA-BZTZ-XXKC
Robin Books Limited
3, The Boundary Lane
Lancashire, L40 5XT, UK.
Tel: 0800 45 85 397
Fax: 0800 45 84 913

A CIP catalogue of this book is available from the British
Library

Typeset in 10/12pt Helvetica by
Derek Doyle & Associates, Shaw Heath
Cover Design by Tudor Print and Graphics, Liverpool
Printed and bound in Great Britain by
St Edmundsbury Press, Bury St Edmunds, Suffolk.

This book is dedicated to the memory of Dale Carnegie, Og Mandino, Norman Vincent Peale, Tai Solarin and Paul Twitchell. They represented my teachers in personal development. I'd like to also dedicate this book to all those who chose and are committed and resolved to create, grow and live a joyful life of abundance.

Contents

ACKNOWLEDGEMENTS

As we say in South West Nigeria, only the sparrow standing on a ridge is bigger than others; only a child sitting on the shoulder of an elder could see farther than other children. I owe the knowledge and wisdom shared in this book to standing on the shoulders of over three thousand other authors and greater teachers and minds, whose company I have enjoyed in the last thirty years. I could not individually acknowledge or thank them without drawing you into my boring old academic world.

Professor Stephen Wilks, I am ever indebted to you for helping me to develop my writing skills and improve my eccentric syntax.

I owe my royal life coach, Steve Slimm, the idea for this book. It is a great business doing pleasure with you! Thank you. You inspire me more than you can ever know. I am thankful to my life coach, Anthony Robbins. Walking with you on coal fire has unleashed the giant within me. I am grateful to Doron Libshtein and Rob Rendle my two coaches on Marketing and Personal Wealth. I am also grateful to all my trainer coaches at the UK Coaching Academy and at the Peter Thomson International. Jonathan Jay, I owe a lot to you and to your team for showing me what I could do as a coach. Peter Thomson, you have been more than my business growth coach but also a mentor. I am grateful to you and to your team. I am grateful to Zik Omope, Jimmy Chapman, Robin Brooks, Steve Critchley and Clive Leach, my great teachers in network marketing.

I am indebted to my coach Jan Nevill for getting me

back to writing, and I owe The New Horizon Group of St Annes, England, for inviting me to give the seminar on which this book developed. I am grateful to all my readers, especially Bams Abila, Ann and Emmanuel Aggrey, Aramide, Kehinde and Taiwo Dauda, Toyin Falola, Dayo Idowu, Zik Omope, Bernard Pepper, Jan Nevill and Elizabeth Wiredu.

Ben Doyle, I am grateful for your contribution to my books. I always appreciate your input not only in type-setting but as a valued friend. Thanks Ben.

I am grateful to my family and friends who have supported me and kept me from giving up in my own dark nights. May the blessings be!

INTRODUCTION

I have written this book especially as my contribution to prepare everyone for the silent revolutions of our time. The old paradigms of full employment, conventional businesses, secured jobs for life, and of state-sponsored social welfare are either inadequate or no longer relevant for our time. Demographic changes, changes in social values and beliefs and technological advancements make such policies as official secrecy totally and absolutely unsustainable.

Our educational systems are informed, designed and constructed on the premise of hierarchical structures of family, religious, social, political and economic institutions. Our cultural institutions were modelled after the pyramid structure. Even our classrooms and offices were designed for the hierarchy and clearly defined boundaries and roles among individual members of the institutions. Everyone knew his or her place in each of the cultural institutions.

The issues of the twenty-first century can no longer be handled with the cultural institutions of the last century. We need a structural adjustment to accommodate today's global issues. For example dealing with a spread of radiation, global warming, environmental pollution, virus diseases, individual and state terrorism is beyond the capacity of individuals and nation states.

The speed of changes also means that we need a new radical, flexible and pragmatic outlook and institutional structure that can respond to and anticipate change with the same rapidity. Our educational systems and cultural institutions do not prepare us to cope with the level of changes we have experienced in the last thirty years. They do not even prepare us to live in a global village.

This book is the outcome of many years of my personal efforts to grapple with the changes and also to support people who want to make sense of the changes. I also hope the book will help people to mentally prepare themselves for the change and hence be able to plan a new life of abundance. I believe that understanding of the dynamics of what is going on is useful for those who are committed to give up poverty and drudgery as a way of life. I define poverty and drudgery as doing a job you hate, despise and loathe.

This book is also about my own journey out of poverty into abundance.

I have studied and tasted poverty and lived the life of poverty and I didn't like it. I have in the process questioned the unfairness of nature, of government policies, and many other explanations available from social science research and literature. In hindsight, I realised I was looking in the wrong direction.

My conclusions are that poverty and abundance could not be explained either by socialism and communism or capitalism. Socialism and communism cannot distribute what it has not produced and capitalism without human face cannot guarantee joy and happiness. Democracy cannot flourish without spiritual awareness, mutual respect and responsibility of the organic link and the global bond between individuals and society. And before we subscribe to crimes either in the name of God or democracy, we must always bear in mind that Adolf Hitler was democratically and legitimately elected as head of state in Germany!

My study started with changing the subject of study. I stopped studying poverty and shifted to studying abundance. I stopped studying the poor and I started researching the life and mentality of the rich.

Consequently, I changed my attitude to money and I made a radical change of my beliefs and values. And when I found out that I am a product of many years of social conditioning and that my habits had been so engraved in my nature, I ended up walking on coal fires and also burnt my bridges to interrupt my old patterns.

You do not need to go as far as I have to start living a life of abundance. You do not need to experience the same level of trauma that I have experienced. You also do not need to wait until you are fifty-five to make such change, and since it is never too late to start, neither do you need to give up if you are already above fifty-five. You simply need to stretch yourself out of your comfort zone.

Simply make a decision, commit yourself to a new lifestyle and be prepared to do whatever it takes; starting now, where you are and with what you have!

Use this book as a reference and companion. Spend time to think through each message and to practise the precepts. It may take about three to seven years of total commitment to bring a total change in your life. Be patient. Keep your present job and make constant and consistent never-ending improvement, and you will be surprised by how your life will transform within a short time.

Develop four blocks of ninety-day plan for each year for the next ten years. We all overrate what we could do in one year and underrate what we could achieve in ten years. Manage and budget your time for each project in each area of your life based on blocks of ninety days at a time. Forty blocks for a period of ten years will give you a sustainable life of abundance.

Whatever your personality type, ninety days are long enough to keep your momentum and energy on a project. Daily, weekly, monthly and quarterly review and monitoring of your progress will keep you on track. Commit yourself to ninety-day programme and make sure you keep working your plan everyday just as you eat everyday. Make plans, monitor and review them and keep your eyes on the prize, on your mission, and on your dream.

Break each task into chunks, and keep taking a step at a time and keep moving. Write that book with one character at a time; climb that mountain with one step at a time; walk a thousand miles by taking one step at a time; pay that debt consistently over a period of time, and make sure you stop digging when you are in a hole!

And remember that living a life of abundance means a balanced life of joy and happiness. And a balanced life is not a daily life of eight hours of sleep; eight hours of work; and eight hours of other activities. It simply means doing the right thing, at the right time, and in the right way. A life of abundance is a life of service. Ironically, a life of abundance is also a life of crisis and challenges and because crisis brings out the best in us, it is therefore a life of miracles. So have fun and be joyful!

Please note that some of the ideas in this book are contradictory and confusing. That is the nature and reality of using human language to express concepts that are ineffable and beyond the capacity of words. Read them over and over, and contemplate on them within the context they are used, and in time you will catch their true meanings.

The 360° Lifestyle Series is a toolset, a map and a guide to the easy, simple and practical way. It is indeed the way. Each volume in the series is seemingly holistic but in reality it is connected to all others. This is what 360° is all about. It is about your individuality within the overall scheme of things in the entire universe. Each volume has its own identity but the overall message is to promote and simplify an understanding of the ecosystem, simply the web of interconnection and interdependence of the entire universe.

Each volume is a living cell just as you are a living Soul. You as an individual have more cells in your body than the entire population of the world and each cell in your body can be cloned to reproduce more than the world population. The series is the universe. Each cell can live independently on its own.

Each volume is therefore capable of meeting your need at every station you are in the never-ending journey of Soul. Each will help you to choose, create and grow a joyful life for the moment, and when you are ready to move on, it will also link you to another volume that will show you the appropriate steps to take!

And as you grow and unfold in your self awareness you will see the universe with a different viewpoint, the viewpoint of an organic whole with each organ taking full responsibility for performing its own function and yet in an interdependent network and in an interlink-communication web with the other organs. This viewpoint will allow you to operate above the power struggles of the zero-sum game of life and to choose, create and grow a joyful life of harmony, charity and cooperative relationships.

Be patient with your existing world view. You are too vulnerable at the beginning. Associate with like-minded people and test the ground before you offend the old order. They have vested interest in the world they knew, and they are too frightened of change. Silence is golden, until you are confident and skilful in handling the dangers, and oftentimes the opportunities!

There is however a good news for you. The world is getting better and more receptive to new ideas and alternative ways of thinking and doing things. Share your insights, experiences and joy with others who are open and receptive. Pass the word around. The easiest way to learn is to teach what we need to learn. Teach and transmit the message. The more you talk about your insights the clearer they become. You will be amazed by how many people are ready and waiting out there for this message.

The style is unusual because the challenges of our time are new. Even typesetting in modern font is part of the process of coming to terms with change. Presenting it as random thoughts is also a strategy to break away from the old structural way of writing a book. We all think randomly and you would have had many flashes of things you needed to do since you started reading this book. That is what 360° Lifestyle is all about. It is about being real, simple and practical.

Keeping it simple, brief and light is part of the overall strategy to climb to the peak of the mountain so that we could see clearly with the bird's eye view. It is always easier to see far when you are at the peak. And if you want to fly high and see far as an eagle you may want to keep away from the companies of turkeys and chickens whose idea of flying is getting on the curb!

Cultivate a beautiful mind. A beautiful mind is a para-chute, it works only when it is open. A beautiful mind is a garden. As the flowers of the garden unfold they give and receive sweet nectar of pleasure and energy. They also invite and attract the beautiful butterflies, bees and other creatures to their world. They connect and are connected with life. They radiate beauty. A life of abun-dance is a beautiful life of joy and service.

Enjoy your new 360° Lifestyle!

LIVING A LIFE OF ABUNDANCE

1. Thank you for being here!
May I return you a favour?

I believe when we discover something of great value, it is our obligation and pleasure to share it with others. I found out the principles of living a joyful life and my mission is therefore to share them with you. They are easy, simple and practical ways. I do hope you choose these principles to create and grow a joyful life for yourself and your loved ones.

I would like to thank you for being my guests. You have done me a great favour and I sincerely and truly feel honoured and privileged. I take your investment of effort, time and money as a sign that you are prepared, committed, determined and willing **to do whatever it takes** to succeed. I congratulate you and commend your effort.

2. Be prepared to do whatever it takes

Whether you knew it or not, you have demonstrated one of the great secrets and mental attitude of living a life of abundance. The highest and indeed the least common factor to everyone and I mean everyone (I have not seen an exception to this group of people) who lives a life of abundance is the preparedness, commitment and resolution to do whatever it takes to succeed.

Maybe the best way to start is to ask, what is a life of abundance? A life of abundance is a life of meaning. And what is a life of meaning? A meaningful life is a life of connection, charity, love and joy. It is a life of freedom and also a rich life. And how do we grow a meaningful life? We grow a meaningful life with extraordinary service? What is an extraordinary service? An extraordinary service is any mindful act, word or thought that brings mutual joy and value to all parties involved. It is mindfully or consciously and regularly seizing any opportunity and chance to use words, thoughts and actions to add value to our lives and the lives of others. It is doing ordinary things in extraordinary ways.

And this brings me to the concept of **Aikido** principle. Aikido is a Japanese phrase, not a word. It is made up of **Ai** (mutual) + **ki** (mind) + **do** (way). There is no equivalent for the phrase in English language. The word mutual for example is not simply an agreement between two persons but an agreement between human beings and the universe. Aikido is therefore the way of harmony between human beings and the universe.

It is based on the premise that no one can attack the universe without losing, and consequently no one can attack you when you are in unity and harmony with the universe. Aikido is a self-defence martial art of making use of the attacker's own movements without causing injury. Because Aikido artists do not inflict any injury on themselves and others, they refer to themselves as players.

My return favour and gift to you is that, with the Aikido principles, it is quite possible for you to choose, create and grow a life of abundance without causing any injury on yourself and others. But like all arts, you need appropriate and adequate attitude, knowledge and skills to play the game of life.

Consistency and a regular practice or patience in action; discipline or persistence in action; and service or love in action will give you confidence, competence and composure to build a life of abundance. Stop fighting life and start understanding life and you would have built a strong foundation for living a life of abundance.

3. Abundance or excuse: which one do you prefer?

You are not in want or need: you already have abundance. Your choice to attend personal improvement and development programmes and to read books is a giant first step to living the life of abundance. To live a life of abundance begins with appreciation and acceptance of what you already have. **You are already enough!** Take for example the gift of life itself and the endowments of creativity, imagination and choice, not to mention the gift of time, space and energy. Yes, you may not have money or materials and I will come to how to generate wealth later. You are already blessed, endowed and gifted with all the potentials it takes to live a life of abundance. The challenge for most of us is that we don't realise it. We are not aware of our potentials, endowments and talents.

Many people believe that they have no time. But we all know that both the queen and the pauper have twenty-four hours a day! If anything the unemployed people and the retired have all the time! **They have excuses but you have time and you are reading this book**.

Making, creating and manufacturing excuses is the main thing holding us back from being who we are and who we could be. You cannot make excuses and create wealth and abundance at the same time. You either take action and create abundance or make excuses and create poverty. For many their excuses are lack of money and energy left after the day's work. You are already living the life of abundance with your decision and choice to invest in your personal growth and I congratulate you.

4. What is your greatest priority?

Successful people are clear about their priorities and they are dogged and ruthless – not in a nasty way – in pursuit of their potentials and priorities. Your choice, your priority, your determination, your focus and your joy to live as if **you already have enough** is the first step to live the life of abundance. Enjoy it.

Excuse yields poverty and scarcity, action yields wealth and abundance.

5. Live only on principles instead of personality

How committed are you to a principled life? Give yourself a score on the scale of one to ten; where ten is a total commitment and one is a little or no commitment?

Will you commit yourself from this moment and for the rest of your life to live a principled and purposeful life? Most of our conflicts arise from our inability to connect with others. We make things personal and we pursue personality. We separate ourselves from the whole. **Keep your life light and simple** and commit to nothing personal and nothing serious and you would have removed most of your head and heart aches!

My experience is that a commitment of less than seven means nothing will ever happen. A commitment of less than seven means your present lifestyle is meeting some of your needs, especially the basic needs for food, shelter, security and warmth. You are not ready to trade off the security of that need, whatever it is, for a new life.

6. Let's have a celebration exercise!

You don't have to do this exercise but I will appreciate your doing it with joy and from your heart. May I request you to face the next person to you; announce your commitment to live from now on with gratitude and appreciation for all the abundance you have in your life; and let the first person congratulate you with a hug!

And then let the second person give a similar commitment, and you now congratulate and give a hug in return. If you are reading this book on your own, give yourself a pat on the shoulders, and put a smile on your face. Well done. You deserve it.

That is your side of the deal? What is my side and what is the catch? When you have a commitment of seven and above, I want to promise you that, from now on, your life will never be the same for you again.

With your total commitment and resolution you can cross the bridge from scarcity to abundance; move from the bridge of poverty to wealth; and pass over from the bridge of failure to success. Please stay on course.

What gives me confidence to make this promise? I am making this promise because I have witnessed and observed the dramatic and sometimes miraculous influence and impact of these secrets and principles on people who have abundance in their lives.

7. Fear is the root of all procrastination

Behind and underlying your discomfort and procrastination are the fears of uncertainty and the uninsurable risk of the unknown! And I have good news for you.

The cure for fear is not to overcome it but to live above it. Identify your fear; name it, for example, anxiety and apprehension against danger or pain for loss; understand its message which is either warning of danger or regrets for the past; face its message with appropriate perspectives and with service or love in action.

You will do well to acknowledge the warnings of danger and to take necessary precautions to address them. Your fear is fuelled and empowered by the attention you give it. Divert your attention from fear and doubts to what you want in your life and what you can do to get it.

Develop faith and belief in yourself and become an Aikido player in the game of life and remember that Aikido players do not injure their attackers.

8. The timeless ancient wisdom for today

Some of you might have come across the secrets and principles in different shapes and forms but I will simplify them for you. They are simple but don't let their simplicity deceive you.

They are different from the shapes you might have previously encountered. They will come to you with greater power, energy and meaning than you have previously associated with them. You will realise the hidden treasure and the magnificent blessings they hold more than you ever did.

They may appear as small as a mustard seed or an acorn or a little figure 0, but they have the pungent power of mustard, the magnificence of an oak tree and the infinite power of figure 0. They will transform your life beyond your dreams and expectations when you let them!

I would like you to take notice of them because they are vintage wine that I have pressed and distilled from the best grapes and particularly from the richest vineyards of wisdom. You can even get copies for your friends and family. It may do you a lot of good to get it for your real and perceived enemies! Now let us get to business.

9. Are you existing or living?

I would like to start with a few comments on 'living', 'life', and 'abundance'. For many of us, we mistake or misunderstand living with existing or earning or learning to live. To exist is simply to follow the basic motions of eating, sleeping, recreating, reproducing and reacting to stimuli of irritation, pain and pleasure. That is what it is to exist. We are simply meeting the needs for bed, bread and butter.

Living demands more than existing. Living requires choosing, planning, planting and growing, creating and having, being, feeling and experiencing, connecting or loving, and contributing and leaving a legacy.

Dinosaurs became extinct because of their failure to anticipate and adapt to change. Living involves not only constantly learning to improve the quality of life for ourselves and for others but also consistently anticipating, embracing and regenerating change and innovation.

I think the best definition of living is from Eleanor H. Porter in her 1913's classic book: *Pollyanna* coined from Polly and Anna. Pollyanna the eleven-year old girl and the main character defines living as 'doing the things you want to do: playing outdoors, reading (to myself, of course), climbing hills, talking to Mr Tom in the garden, and Nancy [the housemaid], and finding out all about the houses and the people and everything everywhere all through the perfectly lovely streets I came through yesterday. That's what I call living, Aunt Polly. Just breathing isn't living!'

The Pollyanna game of positive and mental attitude now has the same derogatory image as money. Many of us would now easily and wrongly parrot-quote that money is the root of all evil, but was that the original text and context? Many of us now would relate to

Pollyanna as simply burying our head in the sand under the pretext of positive thinking, but was that the original context of the game?

Should you have been misinformed and ill-educated as I have been about Pollyanna: 'the just-being-glad game', I would like to recommend you find time to read this book that not only brought tears to my eyes but changed my attitude, perception and life for ever. Seek the truth, and it would definitely liberate and set you free!

10. Become aware and responsible for your life

Living is learning and growing. Learning propels flexibility, adaptability and responsiveness to change. Awareness enables us to take responsibility for all aspects of our life. We learn when we review, record and measure our progress and keep track of what we are doing, where we are, and what we are getting in relation to our desired results.

We are living when we are aware of changes taking place in our global village, when we are proactively able to anticipate, plan, create and grow to accommodate changes around us, when we are patient and flexible to think creatively and constructively to meet changes.

Sanity requires that we change direction and action, when where we are heading to is not the desired destination; when what we are getting is not what we would love to have; and above all when who we are becoming is not in congruence with who we are and who we would love to be. Madness is doing the same thing, in the same old way, and expecting a different result.

11. A purposeful life of becoming is a life of abundance

Find your purpose and mission in life; develop a plan to pursue your dream, purpose and mission in life; commit, resolve, dedicate and focus all your heart and talents to the pursuit of your purpose in life, and you'll forever live in abundance!

Have a purpose and be alive.

The only unforgivable sin of disservice to yourself and to others is stagnation and immobility. Be stiff and you are dead. Be mobile and you are alive and living.

Keep moving and living your purpose and dream!

12. What is the ultimate purpose of life?

The ultimate purpose of life is the experience and expression of joy and happiness often associated with having or meeting our needs or others needs. The more ordinary the need we met, the greater the joy and happiness that comes with it.

For example I could become a millionaire tomorrow but I would always appreciate the gift of fifty pence from my brother in-law because I was able to go to my first cinema with that gift of fifty pence in 1970! I was able to buy bread for my family of six with a gift of five pounds from a friend in 1985! And a hug and a two-hundred-pound loan from my supervisor saved my life in 1988! There are many of such gifts and gestures in my life!

Counting your blessings and playing the just-being-glad game are the greatest sources of energy to live in the turbulent storms, but neutral events in life. You are living when you are either meeting your own needs or the needs of others. Make a gift to yourself or to others.

Such needs range from basic needs for food, shelter and warmth to emotional needs for love, recognition and security, and the spiritual needs for growth, contribution and leaving a legacy.

The peak moments of meeting human needs are often experienced or expressed with feelings of satisfaction, relief, security, freedom, accomplishment, achievement, recognition, importance, and sometimes with spiritual feelings of unity, wholeness, connection or love, union or re-union, contribution, leaving a legacy or a living memory of immortality!

So how do we meet our ultimate personal needs for joy and happiness?

13. What is your life now: A barren desert or an oasis?

How does one create a life of abundance? Please note that this is the most confusing and difficult part about using words to express ideas. Human languages are inadequate to present ideas and I'll do my best to simplify this contradicting complex idea. Once you understand the irony, the simplicity and the spirit and soul of this idea your life is changed for the better.

You create wealth and abundance and live a life of abundance not by working long hours, not by working harder or smarter, not by cheating or being clever but simply with effortless effort, doing without doing and being in harmony and balance with yourself and your environment. Be in unity with the universe.

Creative and constructive ideas for wealth and abundance do not grow in the barren, stressful and overcrowded gardens and fields of drudgery.

They flourish in the fertile oasis and in the relaxed, leisurely and luxurious recess golf fields. They are conceived and generated behind the lonely and solitude writing desks and the experimenting backyard work-shops of inventors. They are consistently, persistently and patiently pursued in the recreational fields of hobby addicts, and they are nurtured with the obsessive and passionate labour of love of entrepreneurs! And what do I mean?

14. What is the formula to create a purposeful life?

All the little effort it takes is to identify whatever gives you personal joy and happiness, whatever you are interested in so much that it makes you feel complete, whole and connected. Find out what wakes you up? Discover what gives you a buzz, what gives you energy?

Your birthday for living the life of abundance is the day you find what you are connected with and what you are ready to pay for in order to be able to do it, to have it, and to be it. Your next challenge is to find people who need products or services, that is, what you love to do, to have and to be, and who are ready to pay for it.

Study, learn, experiment and do whatever it takes to find what you love to be and woo and keep the company of people who are willing to pay you, and you will have discovered the diamond fields of wealth.

Immerse, commit and dedicate your life to develop your field of interest and abundance is guaranteed as your reward for the investment of your time, energy, money and space.

Figuratively set yourself on fire with passion and enthusiasm for your field of interest, and people would pay to watch you burn!

15. Boredom is one of our greatest endowments: Recognise it and use it!

Watch out for, and respond to, the red lights and alarm signals in your life! Your body is designed to function effectively. Your body, like your car or any machine, has built-in signals to warn and alert you of how it is performing and functioning. You have all forms of emotions with different signals of how things are going inside. The problem is we ignore the signals until our body and mind can take it no longer and give up on us or break down.

The universal acid test to know when you are short-changing yourself in life is boredom. **Boredom is the thermostat to give you a nudge that you could be more, achieve more and indeed do better with your life.**

Must we be burnt-out before we respond to the smoke alarm? Must we have a stroke or a heart attack before we slow down to reduce stress and bring down our rising blood pressure?

Must we become depressed before we respond to boredom? We are bored when we are not engaged in any venture that can meet or add value to our purpose for expression and experience of joy in life.

Boredom is often associated with disconnection, stagnation and a lack of fulfilment. It is a simple and an effective alarm signal that we are short-changing ourselves in life. It is a common factor of under perfor mance and neglect of our mission, dream or purpose in life. It is nature's wake-up call to do more for ourselves and for the rest of the universe.

It is impossible to be bored and at the same time to experience any joy or happiness. So why not decide to use the gift of boredom and the moment of boredom to transform your life? It doesn't matter what your situation or circumstance in life is at the moment. It really does not matter how old and how poor you are. All it requires is to begin to ask the right question! What can I do now to add value to my life? What can I do now to add meaning to my life? What can I do now to make the difference to myself and to others?

Sometimes it is difficult to come up with new ideas. If your situation or circumstance is so underwhelming, simply relate, re-associate and reconnect yourself with the last time you were happy and joyful, excited and alive! What were you doing? Where were you? What were you feeling? Seeing? Or hearing? Re-live the experience, again and again!

Whatever answer you arrive at, begin now to re-live the experience even in your imagination. The mind does not know the difference between reality and imagination. Start now. Do it now, where you are now. The acre of diamonds is right where you are now. Begin to mine it, now!

16. It is never too late

It is never too late to start living in abundance. Ask yourself whether you are absolutely happy and satisfied with your life? What is best in your life at the moment; what you would like to improve in your life; who you are at the moment; who you would love to be, if you were assured and guaranteed to succeed; what regrets you have in life; what your dreams were when you were seven years old; and who you loved to be when you were seven years old?

We need to revisit our lives at seven because most of us had perfect dreams of who we really love to be when we were seven! What went on between seven and now? Are you living your dreams or are you living the lives planned for you by your parents, by society or by your peers?

The good news is that **it is never too late to start**. And that is one of the secrets of people who have lived a life of abundance.

They woke up one day and they decided to follow their dreams. Only a few people lived all their lives with abundance. Indeed only a few ever started living in abundance before they were forty years old. Most people started in their fifties and sixties.

The bad news and the only saddest thing is when it is on our deathbeds that we wished we had become the person we loved to be, and that we had not neglected our dreams, purpose and mission.

17. Make a decision and you change your destiny and shape your future

Let this moment be your moment of awakening. Let this moment be a moment of **decision, commitment and action**.

It is in this moment of decision that we change our destiny.

Let this moment be the turning point in your life. Let it be the moment to begin to live the life of your dream and the moment to become the person we desire to be!

You were born to be happy and joyful. Make a decision now to experience joy and happiness and reconnect yourself with the ultimate purpose of your being.

You have the power to choose and it is your birthright to choose joy and happiness. You exercise your birthright only when you experience or express joy, happiness and connection.

You can decide to choose joy, happiness and connection now.

Expressing and experiencing connection now and

always is a choice and you can make that choice now. It is in the moment of decision and choice that we shape our future and change are destiny.

18. Is success a sly fox or a goddess of luck?

There are different names for the beast of success. Some say it is a sly beast, like a fox, slipping in when and where not expected. I am not quite sure about that assessment and I'll explain my objection.

It is a drill and definitely as all drills, it requires practice, patience, study, anticipation, rigour and vigour. Success requires courage. It is definitely not for the feeble-minded and the weak. It requires sweating it out consistently and persistently.

The alchemist of success is the good mix of ideas, thoughtfulness and actions, and the meeting of inspiration with preparation and perspiration. It is estimated that success is one percent inspiration and ninety-nine percent preparation, perspiration and tenacity.

Some would like us to believe that success is a goddess of luck smiling and granting favours to those who do her bidding! Maybe they are right, but they are only right if LUCK is the acronym for *Labour Under Correct Knowledge.*

Who are you and who do you love to be? Take a few moments to write down who you believe you are now and who you want to be! Make a solemn commitment to yourself never to settle for less than you can be!

Commit and resolve to live up to your potentials and dreams.

19. You woke up the wild lion and rocked the boat of entropy!

We all want to live and remain in a state of rest and equilibrium. It is natural law. It has different names: comfort zone, state of rest or state of equilibrium. When a force is pressed on any matter or on us either to push or pull it or to push or pull us out of equilibrium or comfort zone, entropy, the second law of thermodynamics, is set in motion. There is chaos, confusion or commotion.

And that exactly is what happens when you commit yourself to wake up, to move out of your comfort zone, and to pursue your dream, purpose or mission in life. Two things will happen and I want to take you through the two so that you know what to expect and how to handle them.

The first is a hard one and it defeats most people. The second is the mythical miracle, the glorious dawn that often followed the dark night of the Soul, a stillness and calmness after a turbulent storm of obstacles and failed attempts. Only few people pass the first series and waves of obstacles, challenges, and defeats to experience the series of events conspiring to support our mission, purpose and dreams beyond our expectations.

The first thing is the most difficult and most people give up and quit before the second thing could happen. They never had the opportunity to experience the miracle. Ironically most people who want to change their lives make the same mistakes and hence not only do they make the first hurdle more difficult, they also fail to reduce its impact.

The impact of the first hurdle is so traumatic and stressful that most people regret the move, retreat and withdraw to the known and the seemingly secure old ways.

Many are so crushed by defeat and so frightened

that they never have the courage to try again. They accept their lot. They quit and delude themselves with security. They resign to the so-called secure life of fear, mediocrity and drudgery.

Unfortunately for most failures, they do not realise that the gatekeeper of success would not allow any fraud to enter. All victors are tested for their clarity of purpose, for their sincerity of commitment, for their doggedness of determination and discipline, and for their readiness and willingness to pay the gate fees of sweat, consistency, patience and flexibility.

Keep your eyes on the prize! Keep going and keep moving! Keep doing what failures would not do, and indeed what you have to do and must do to succeed but you wouldn't like to do!

They are the sacrifices, the opportunity costs and the gate fees to success, pay them and enjoy the rewards, the prizes and the desired results. The reality of our times is that whether or not you rock the boat, the boat is capsizing, and you may as well enjoy the brakes and the splashes of the waves while relying on your inner strength to see you through the storms!

20. Life is a coin of crisis: One side is danger and the other side is opportunity

Life is a duality of opposites. The reality of life is that you cannot have a coin without both sides. Success and freedom is the other assured side of obstacles and failures. Each side is separated only by fear and united by love. With consistency, courage, positive attitude, skills and knowledge fear retreats for success and freedom to come into your life.

What follows your decision to live a life of abundance?

Obstacles! Obstacles!! Obstacles!!!

Series of objections, rejections and obstructions confront you from all angles. Your moments of blissful ignorance are now suddenly flooded with confusion and other forms of knowledge indigestion.

Your tested, proven and engraved old habits, beliefs and values, often group-directed and socially approved ways, are now in clash, confrontation and conflicts against your new fragile personal purpose and mission, unproven, untested and doubtful beliefs, albeit higher values and standards.

21. Learn to handle the dark nights of the Soul

You drain your energy and time on the internal struggle between the old and the new sets of beliefs and paradigms. You struggle to refuel your enthusiasm; tenacity and audacity to bypass your old world of scarcity and to establish the new world of abundance. This means that you overload yourself with too much too soon, and you develop indigestion.

Your circle of influence in the new life is so small that it is easily possible that you are crushed and frustrated before you have any breakthrough. I've since developed a formula to effect change in your life with little or no trauma. I call it stretching instead of jumping!

Be aware of this critical moment. Learn to recognise the moments of the dark night of the Soul. It is the moment when your seed is germinating. Relax and be patient and gentle with yourself at this crucial moment. Recognise and accept your feelings of discomfort and confusion. Be still and keep the law of silence. This moment will pass.

22. Stretch don't stress: the change management formula

Stretch yourself out of the comfort zone. This formula requires you to break the pattern without burning the bridge or walking on fire. It requires that you break your habits and raise your standards without violently breaking away from your friends and family. It requires you to understand life instead of fighting life. It requires building a team without breaking away from the old team. I'll come back to this in a moment. First let me illustrate the first thing to expect with my experience before and after I walked on coal fire.

23. Before and after I walked on coal fire and burnt my bridge!

I have burnt my bridges a few times in life. I could recall moving from Nigeria to Britain; giving up my secure job in the civil service to pursue my ambition to become a professor; giving up my secure job as a university head of department to become a taxi driver and giving up taxi driving to become a life coach and a full-time writer. My belief is simply that of burning the bridge and facing the unknown with energy, focus and determination. I was very much a surgeon!

Yes I believe there are occasions when our situation in life gives us the choice between a surgeon and a physician! A surgeon believes in, or is rather trained in the art of, cut and go, a quick fix. Took you in to amputate the left leg; and somehow made a mistake and cut off the right leg. Got you out of theatre and realized that he had cut the healthy right leg and returned you into the theatre to cut the left leg and you end up with no legs. I hope you don't get me wrong here! I have nothing against surgeons.

On the other hand you have the physician with the patience of let's do as many tests as possible. Let's wait and see what medication will do the trick.

There are good times and places for either a surgeon or a physician in our lives. The question and the great challenge you and I will continue to face in life is to determine, know and choose when either surgery or patience is appropriate.

Sometimes the most appropriate way to break certain habits and patterns is to do an outrageous thing such as walking on coal fires or to burn the bridge! And on some occasions the best is the gentle and gradual process of stretching and expanding your circle of influence.

24. The right time is now

Only you can tell what is most appropriate for your circumstance, but remember this next secret to living a life of abundance is that the time is never right. **The right time is now**. Do what you know where you are now and with what you have now. When you know better, then, by all means do better. But do something right now. What you do where you are now determines and shapes your destiny and future.

I burnt my bridge again after I walked on the coal fire. I left taxi driving.

Our unfulfilled dreams, mission and purpose in life don't go away. We cannot wish them away. We could deny and delay them but they have the capacity to reincarnate. We need to recognise them and deal with them. Unlearnt lessons also have the same pattern. They mutate and reincarnate.

Because I left my old jobs without securing new ones to move to I suffered the consequences of my recklessness.

25. What good could come out of crisis?

But there is something good from it. In the process I developed the principle of stretching instead of jumping. I recommend stretching because it is more natural, enduring and sustainable and absolutely less stressful and traumatic than jumping.

To move from A to B, take a little step at a time. Instead of jumping, keep moving. Take one step at a time. Keep removing the weeds from your life. Keep improving your character. Keep stretching and expanding your areas of influence, knowledge and skills.

Remember that Fear means *False Evidence Appearing Real*.

Learn the laws of success and observe them.

Study success and the systems for success, adopt, adapt and apply them to create your own success. Luck is the ability and capability to study, seek, recognise, create and seize chance opportunity.

26. Only you can determine who you are and what you get in life

Now, pay a particular attention to this point. It is one of the greatest secrets of successful people. It is also the secret of most of the dramatic changes you see in people. Most people who have transformed their lives have done so with this little secret I am going to share with you. Your life too will change the moment you accept this simple point of fact and principle of success.

Your life and destiny are determined by this simple fact. Your lot in life; your state and status in life; your circumstance and indeed your destiny in life is not determined by the state of the economy; not governed by the government in power and their policies; not predetermined by your parents and your genetic and biological makeup! Your destiny is not determined by your gender, sexual orientation, race, creed, religion, social class or background.

You are who you believe you are and you can only rise to the standard you set for yourself. You can only consistently be who you think and believe you are.

27. Simply break the pattern: be the wise third little pig

Let me take you back to your childhood and the moral of the story of the three little pigs and the wolf.

The first little pig built a house of straw and the wolf huffed and puffed and blew down the house of straw and killed and had the first little pig for dinner.

The second little pig repeated a similar mistake by building a house of wood and was also killed and eaten up.

The wise third little pig stopped to think, to study the pattern, to learn and to act on its findings. The wise third little pig looked around and decided to model humans who had brick houses and were safe from the threat of lions. And so the third little pig spent some time to build a brick house and the hungry wolf huffed and puffed and could not blow down the brick house!

To change your life may not take as much as Ninety Days as some authors have claimed and promised. It may not take as much as seven days or indeed seven minutes nor as much as it took me to walk on the coal fire that was burning at 2000° Celsius.

It may only take as long as it takes you to switch on or switch off the light. And it would only take as long as it takes you to change your beliefs and raise your standards and values.

For some people it takes the winking of an eye! For me it took me over fourteen years of study and practice, but the real change took about twenty seconds of walking on coal fire!

Just become the wise third little pig. Learn to identify the pattern and be ready to model the successful human neighbours of the wise third little pig. It didn't go out to re-invent the wheel, it just **modelled and duplicated** housing patterns of the humans and built its brick house that was safe from the trial and errors of its siblings. Learn to model and to duplicate success, and to associate and to anchor yourself with the successful people.

28. Align what you do with who you are

This is the most important and of course the most frightening part of this secret: **You will do everything to live within your beliefs and values or standards**. You will consistently be who you believe you are. And I would like to emphasize this point.

You will be restless and uncomfortable to operate lower than your standards and you will do everything possible to sabotage yourself to implement anything that is not consistent with your beliefs and values.

Align yourself with what you do, who you are and who you are becoming.

Align your private life with your public life, your family life and your work, career and professional life.

Align your thoughts and ideas with your internal dialogue and actions.

Align your mind, body and spirit. Align your past, present and future. Get a life coach to work with you to assess, redesign and get your wheel of life in motion.

Let's examine occasions when you have succeeded in life! Let's go back in time and examine when you were happy and everything went well for you! Who were you with? Did they share the same values as you? Did they share the same standards and beliefs as you? Did you have the same interests? Did you feel connected with them? Did you know them, trust them and like them? You could do the same exercise for when things were not going well for you!

To live the life of abundance is to seek to know who you are, be who you are and give back to life. **Consistency, congruency and harmony between who you are and who you love to be** are the greatest secrets to live the life of abundance.

Poverty is living a life of separation, disconnection and gap between who you are and who you believe you love to be.

Abundance is doing what you love to do; having what you love to have; when you love to have it; and being who you are; and who you always love to be.

And the most powerful ten two-letter words are: **If it is to be, it is up to me!**

29. Beware of the questions you ask

You start to ask the right and empowering questions of possibilities and necessities. What can I do to help you? What do I have to learn in this experience? What is for the good of all in this decision? Is it fair and for the good of all? Is it the right thing to do? Is it the right time to do it? Is it the right way to do it? Is there a better time, place or way to do it? Could we save time, energy, money and space when we do it differently? How could I improve my communication? How could I make a better and convincing presentation?

And what is the reward and catch for your new attitude? You become receptive, creative and constructive.

You become a genius, a listener and a wise person. You empathise with your enemies and opponents. You allow for benefits of doubts! What if I were on the other side? How would I react if I were a child, a student, a refuge, a migrant, a recipient of bullying? What if? What if and what if I was wrong?

Take the risks of what if? You might discover that the world is not flat! You might discover that we could transmit without wire! And you might discover that broken mirrors could turn your room into colourful rainbows! You might even discover that the darker the night the brighter the stars! But you can only be what you believe you are and what you believe you can be!

So if your beliefs are not meeting your need, you would do yourself a lot of good by changing them. They are furniture and clothes and now and then we outgrow our beliefs. Sometimes we need to upgrade, change and modify some of our beliefs or adjust them to meet the local, national or global changes in beliefs and values. Now and then we need to change the way we express our beliefs in order to be current and politically correct!

Hypocrisy of the extreme political correctness is not my stuff, though!

30. The Aikido player of life

This and only this simple fact is the core to living the life of abundance. When you love and believe in what you are doing, it becomes a **labour of love**. It becomes a pleasure. You do all that it takes. You put in more than is expected of you. You walk the extra mile. You radiate joy in the service. Your body language becomes congruent with your voice. You are in total harmony and unity with yourself and the rest of the universe.

Balance and harmony is not working eight hours,

sleeping eight hours, and playing eight hours. It is congruency between who you are and who you are becoming on the one hand and what you do and say on the other. It is simply doing the right thing at the right time and in the right way.

You are now an *Aikido* player of life. You are in the zone. You are at the peak. You and what you are doing become one. You are congruent with your career, family, recreation, society and the rest of the universe. All aspects of your life are synchronised. You are balanced. You are now doing the right thing, in the right way, and at the right time. You are now not only universal but the universe.

Life now supports you. The universe supports you. And what follows? Miracle begins. The obstacles begin to wither away. You begin to see wonders in your life. Abundance flows your way and into every aspect of your life. **You become lucky!** You are enlightened, abundant and enough!

And when you take some time to reflect, you look around you, and take account of the number of people you started with, you realize that only few people are with you. You look into how you got from there to here and you are humbled. The majority are down at the bottom of the ladder and there are a few struggling to get to the top. They had given up too early before getting to the peak. They quit and because quitters never won, winners never quit.

31. Values and beliefs: Review your beliefs and values and raise your standards

At any time we have lots of beliefs, some of them are limiting and some are empowering. Most of them we chose by default. We inherited them from the agents or institutions of socialisation: our family, schools, peer groups, and religious and occupational institutions.

What are your beliefs about materials? We measure materials with money. So what are your beliefs about money? Is money the root of all evil or the lack of money the root of all stress, *dis*-ease and evil? Will you say money is a means of exchange? What are your beliefs about time? What are your beliefs about energy? What are your beliefs about space? Do you believe the world is over populated?

What is a perfect way to start? Become a gardener and a farmer of your own secret gardens. Cultivate new habits, beliefs and values. Raise the bar of your standards. Remember that we cannot solve a problem with the same level of consciousness that created it in the first place. Most people believe that the grass is greener on the other side, and I always say yes, but it is only because there are better gardeners on the other side!

When you are ready to grow a new lifestyle, do what the farmers and gardeners do. Decide and choose what seeds and plants you want in your new garden and fields. Prepare the ground and fields. Uproot the old plants and in this case the old habits and patterns. Study the soil and replace it where necessary and appropriate! Learn and practise to be a better gardener and you'll have a greener grass.

32. Plan your life and be a finisher: follow through your plans

Plan your life! Prepare for your life and act on your plan. Be disciplined. Walk the fire and burn the bridge and do whatever it takes to live the new lifestyle. Begin with a plan and design to live a life of abundance. Patiently plough your way through to becoming who you really love to become.

I could hear you groaning, asking, yes that is easily said with your doctorate degree! But where do I start? I've no money, no capital, no education and I have no qualifications! I am too old or I have all the children to feed, the mortgage and the bills to pay, and all the responsibility.

But is that all there is to life and what life is all about? Of course that is an aspect of what life is about. It only becomes a challenge when these duties and responsibilities are pursued as an end in themselves as opposed to being a means to meeting the ultimate desire and purpose to express and experience joy, happiness and connection.

And that takes us to the next secrets of living the life of abundance. We are all endowed with all it takes to live the life of abundance. The acre of diamonds is not in our backyard, it is indeed closer. It is right between our two ears!

33. The acres of diamonds are right between our two ears!

You are endowed with the greatest computer on earth. You carry between your two ears an infinite and unlimited powerhouse of memory, imagination, vision and creativity. Your brain is your greatest asset. Your brain is indeed an invaluable intellectual capital. Use it. Develop it. Explore and exploit it to your advantage.

Neurological research has confirmed that no one has ever used five percent of the brain. Yet application of a little fraction of the brain has created symbols that enabled me to write this book and for you to read it. Application of a fraction of the brain has enabled humans to fly, to invent computers, to organise and to do what our ancestors would have considered as impossible.

What are you doing with your acres of diamonds? When are you going to start mining your diamonds?

When are you going to invest a little time to develop your acres of diamonds? When are you going to plug into the SYSTEMS, and Save Your-Self Time, Energy, Money and Space? One of the greatest secrets of living a life of abundance is the use of your head.

A life of abundance does not come by accident. We dream it. We choose it. We plan it. We plant and grow it. We tend and attend to it. We nurture it. We work, build and create it. We do whatever it takes to build it. Nothing will happen until we make it happen. Massive actions yield massive results.

34. Begin to develop your acres of diamonds

In the last thirty years, virtually everyday, I spent a lot of time, energy and money acquiring information. Most of the space in my home is even devoted to storage of books and information.

I read. I have actually read more than three thousand books in the last thirty years. That is an average of two books a week! I listen to tapes and compact discs and recently I added watching video and digital versatile discs (DVDs). I think and I plan and I become a living encyclopaedia.

Many people refer to me as a wise man. Was I born with knowledge and wisdom? Was I born creative? Not really. Since creativity is receptivity however, I trained my brain to receive, to review, to restore, to recycle and to regenerate ideas.

My brain becomes a nursery home for ideas. I constantly and consistently invest in updating know-ledge, ideas and wisdom. I review, drop or reinvent old ideas.

I derive a special pleasure and satisfaction, enter-tainment and amusement from ridiculous, ludicrous and incredulous old ideas. I regenerate, incubate, mutate, clone, grow and enjoy new ideas.

Hence from growing up as a son of a peasant farmer I have been able to write half a dozen books, to complete my doctorate degree within a record time of two years. The average time is ten years!

I am saying this not to impress you but to impress upon you one of the greatest secrets of living the life of abundance. It is the use of human endowments. It is the use of the power of vision, imagination and creativity. And since you are gifted with vision, imagination and creativity you, too, can choose to turn your life around.

Whatever your mind can conceive and believe, your mind can achieve.

35. Use your powers of vision, imagination and creativity

All inventors and all leaders and all people who live a life of abundance are dreamers, visionaries, missionaries and readers of people, events and, more recently in human history, readers of books. Imagine where to and how far you could travel with your imagination, vision and your favourite authors! No limits to the illusionary forces of time, energy, matter and space. You are as poor as your vision, imagination, ingenuity and creativity.

Right now, tap into your gifts of vision, imagination and creativity and begin to enjoy the abundance of the universe. There is a lot of fresh air at the top, and a lot of leg room in first class. Be bold and courageous to travel first class. The old days of thinking that you must remain in your place and state in life have proved untenable in Japan where virtually all Japanese believe they belong to the middle class!

The feudal era is gone. We no longer need hewers of

wood and carriers of water. We only need pipes for gas and water, and the cables for electricity!

36. Think outside the box

The only limit to accessing your vision, imagination and creativity is the mental captivity of thinking within the box. But you can train to think. Begin to think outside the box. Whenever it makes sense, break the pattern of social paralysis. And whenever it is not harmful to anyone, challenge the limiting rules and traditions. Without such challenges in the past we would be trading in human beings today!

Travel through a different route to work. Use a different method to solve a problem. Allocate about ten minutes to half an hour to think everyday. Sit in a quiet place with pen and paper and contemplate on an idea. Read books on brain, on how memory works, on how to improve, develop and use your memory and on how to mind-map. Suspend your disbelief for a moment.

Your society, group or family and other educational systems have trained you and conditioned you to do things in a particular way. Just for a change, experiment with opposite approaches and ways of doing things. You will be amazed that most breakthroughs are break away!

Most of the greatest inventors and geniuses were rebels, non-conformists and school dropouts. They day-dreamed and they were bored at school! They were labelled as inattentive, too boisterous and suffering from attention deficit syndrome. I am not encouraging truancy and lawlessness, I am simply asking you to appreciate that thinking outside the box could be the easiest way to solve a knotty problem or bring a fresh idea and a refreshing perspective to an intractable situation.

You cannot live in the rapidly changing global village

without becoming a student of change, anticipating change and innovating with vision, creativity and ingenuity.

Have fun and let me know how you are doing! Most inventions were errors or mistakes to start with.

Maybe you too would be blessed with some wonderful mistakes and errors in your life!

37. Break the bonds of social paralysis

Do you know how elephants are trained, conditioned, and domesticated? It is a simple process of tying them to trees when they are young and powerless such that after fruitless efforts they lose faith in their strength. And they never attempt to try again when they are old and should be strong enough to pull down any tree! You and I have gone through the same conditioning process.

As a baby we were born able to swim! We now need to change or expand our references, and where necessary create or learn new references. Expand your awareness, knowledge and understanding. Most fears are rooted in myths and false evidence, references and assumptions appearing real.

We need to regain our childhood audacity to eat from the dog's bowl without asking the dog's permission. We need to dream as a child. Sleep as a child. Who knows we may even be able to learn new skills and languages like a child. Experiment like a child. It is never too late to wake up and enjoy a life of adventure, fun and creativity just like a child!

38. Recapture the dreams of your childhood

Living a life of abundance means that as children of the new lifestyle we'll apply the childlike attitude of curiosity. Unless you adopt the childlike attitude, you cannot experience and express real joy, happiness and unconditional connection. Like a child, there is need to take nothing personal, to take nothing seriously, and be neither critical nor judgemental.

As children, we need to ask questions with an open mind and with curiosity just to know without any ulterior motive and we need confidently and fairly to empathise, challenge and disagree with others without malice or ill-feelings. We'll like children learn and play and be consistently persistent to have what we consider to be our due. To be a child is to be a kid, a resilient and persistent rather than a stubborn baby goat!

And in using our heads, we'll learn to erase and forget unpleasant experiences, to build and pull down our sand castles, to enjoy our toys and throw them aside and to move on regardless. We'll also learn to tickle and giggle, and to laugh and show our gums after we have traded our milk teeth to the tooth-fairy for fifty pence. And if you have not enjoyed sugar and chocolate-free youth as I did, and now have your 32 teeth growing strong, you could laugh and show your false teeth! And when the day is over we could go to bed and sleep with lullaby and hope of sweet dreams!

Let go of the dead yesterday. Monkeys are caught in Africa by putting nuts in coconut shells. They grip the nuts in the coconut cage and will not let go of the nuts and they are trapped because their fists are now unable to get out of the coconut shells.

My father played a trick on me as a child. He asked me to hold some magical leaves before going to sleep. The leaves were to protect me at night and to drive away any wild animals giving me nightmares. The leaves would have potent protection energy only if they were no longer in my palms when I woke up the following morning.

I must let go of them when I sleep else he would

have to look for another charm to protect me. The following morning, the leaves were indeed no longer in the palms of my hands. Some of the leaves were cooked for me to eat so that harm would never happen to me as I am ever protected after eating them! The rest were burnt and rubbed into razor blade marks that were made around my wrists so that I could have the protection running in my veins. And how could I prove it is not working since I started to sleep better and I am alive!

Don't be a monkey, who wouldn't let go of the bait. Be a child and let go of all your emotions and the trappings of our society!

39. The process of choosing, creating and growing abundance

Let us spend some time with details. Living the life of abundance is a process. It starts with choosing abundance. We humans are all endowed with the power of choice. We have the power to choose, to create and to grow. Angels have no choice; they can only do good!

We also have the power of association and capacity to manage our physiology, language and emotions. Our motions create our emotions and good management of our internal dialogue could dramatically change our reality. We have power of perception and interpretation. We can change our emotions and behaviours simply by changing our perception, the value and the meanings we attach to events and to our experiences. We can adopt new habits and frame of references, beliefs and values.

40. Study the universal laws and observe them

Let us take a moment to examine the four forces of

time, energy, space and matter. What is your attitude to time? Are you relaxed, happy and contented with twenty-four hours? Do you feel you have enough time in the day? Do you want more time? How do you respond to your time? How do you use it?

What are your beliefs about justice? How would you describe life? Will you consider life as a game? If it is a game, is it fair? Is it a no-win game or a zero-sum game, in which someone has to lose for you to win? Do you consider life as a school or a battle field? What determines your assessment of life? What are your beliefs about wealth? We can ask similar questions about space. Is your home crowded? If yes, with what? Is it crowded with what you really need or with junk? What are the cobwebs in your life?

Let us look at the big 'M's, that is, money, matter and materials. Would you consider yourself as rich, wealthy and living in abundance? Do you have things? Do you want things or do you need things? What accounts for your debts? Are they basic needs and essentials or are they luxuries?

What would you consider as luxury? For me luxuries are what would be nice to have but not critical to my survival or existence. Would you die if you were to ride a functional car and work less hours? How would you feel about raising your standards and increasing the quality of your life? What about giving more time and energy to what is important in your life?

The metaphors we use are crucial and important for the way we view things and respond to events. Review your metaphors and where appropriate and necessary, change them. It is a simple and an effective way to transform your life.

Pursuing a meaningful life and spending your time on important things are what Pollyanna would consider to be living and not just breathing. Begin to live today. Tomorrow will never come.

41. Ideas! Ideas!! Ideas!!!
The greatest secret of generating wealth

Simply study and understand the science and system of generating wealth and abundance and your life will never be the same. Stop the struggle and invest time and energy in learning.

Have you come across people who have changed their lives considerably and dramatically within a short period of time? What did they do to accomplish the miracles? How did they change or transform their lives from virtually nothing or rebuild their lives from disaster and ruins? Could anyone do what they did? Yes, I would like to believe.

Now tell me, do you have a friend or know anyone who has suddenly transformed her or his lifestyle? What do you think was done to create the transformation? Do you know how it was done? What was sacrificed to have the new lifestyle? What price was paid? Are you ready to pay the price for a new lifestyle? Is it worth it?

I can hear loud and clear what you are thinking! You are telling me and shouting back at me that you don't have money, capital, means and all the resources to start your business. I know it because I have been there. I know how you feel. I felt that way before, but this is what I found out. I researched to know how millionaires made their money, to know what they went through and what obstacles they confronted and how they surmounted them.

Please go out from here and find out for yourself from any successful corner shop owner to owners of superstores. Ask anyone you consider is living the life of abundance and you will come to know that one and only one thing that accounted for their successes: they had IDEAS. They BELIEVED in themselves and in their ideas, and they COMMITTED to work on their ideas until they succeeded.

Millionaires don't start with money or capital. They start with ideas.

42. Begin to think like a millionaire

Let me share with you the mentality of a millionaire. Please don't get me wrong here. I am a millionaire in training. I am moving close to my first million! I am now closer than before I started writing this book. And it all adds up.

I spent the last seven years researching how millionaires made it and you are having it all in two hours. I experimented for over thirty years and more importantly I spent my time trying to reinvent the wheel. Don't go on that route. It is a waste of time. Just put a new wagon on alloy wheels!

A joyful life of abundance can be as easy or difficult as we make it. A joyful life of abundance will never come if it's a goal in itself; it is a by-product of a commitment to worthy causes and particularly to living a life of service. Just make up your mind to living a life of service.

I am happy for you because you can finish reading this book and become a millionaire within the next five years. First, start believing, living, thinking, acting, working and being a millionaire. A janitor or porter or security officer asked the chief executive of a multinational corporation: 'What does it take to be a chief executive?' The Chief Executive replied, 'Believe you are one, dress like one, move like one, think like one, talk like one, and act like one!' So, I would like to ask you to start thinking and acting like a millionaire.

About five years ago I gave two or three seminars. I do not even remember the topics because I did not think, talk and act like a millionaire. I did not write out the seminars and I did not record them. I did not charge fees for my talk and travel.

That was my old poverty mentality.

43. Expand your awareness or expire

So what has changed for me in the last one year? Many have bought copies of this book and there are copies left for you to buy for your family and friends. When I got the invitation for the seminar, I thought first as an academic, but that was immediately replaced with thinking like a millionaire. I was ready to go and have fun as I used to do as a university lecturer and I would like to think everyone enjoyed it as much as I did.

But lectureship fun is not enough for a millionaire. I could add value and make some money. I started getting ideas. It is not enough to go and talk. I could add value to their evening and mine. The organisers offered a stipend for petrol but that was not enough for me. So I thought I could write my talk and make it into a pamphlet for attendees to buy. What about recording it and make a cassette tape, a compact disc, a digital versatile disc, a video, and what about putting it on the internet for people to download for a fee from my website and what about using it as a chapter in my next book? It is now a book and not just a chapter.

With the value added thinking of a millionaire, I have about seven money-generating products from a two-hour seminar. Yes, it has taken me about ten days to prepare the seminar and about six weeks to rewrite it into a book, but that is it. All the products are now fruits from my MONEY TREE!

The seeds have been planted, nurtured and I can sit back for a never-ending harvesting of royalty. Each time anyone buys it, I get royalty. Sounds simple, but let me give you a bit of warning here. It is about the greatest principle that governs our efforts. It is called the 80/20 principle!

44. Learn and earn with 80/20 principle!

The principle is based on the fact that eighty percent of our efforts give twenty percent of our results. You could stretch the principle to eighty percent of the world own twenty percent of the wealth or twenty percent of your customers would give eighty percent of your profit! Indeed eighty percent of the earth planet is covered by water and eighty percent of the land is covered by desert. You could play and apply the game to anything and to any area of your life!

And what it all comes to is that if you could spend your time to find out and focus your attention on who, when, where, and what constitute that twenty percent you could work less, worry less, succeed more and enjoy more. You do not need to do extraordinary things to get extraordinary results.

But more importantly is the fact that what gives you most joy and happiness in life does not cost you more than twenty percent of your earnings, your time, and your efforts!

I hope you do note and appreciate that you would however have to give one hundred percent concentration, effort and attention to discover the mysterious twenty percent! And that means you would keep on putting in that extra mile, energy, time and everything it takes to succeed. There is always one more step!

45. Think of royalty and multiple residual incomes

Pay yourself first and let your money work for you. Divide your time between the short term security of working for money and the long term programme for financial freedom through employing money to work for you.

Interest on savings and capital, dividends on invest-

ments, licence fees on franchises, rent on properties, royalty on intellectual property, and commission on referrals are examples of residual income.

The simplest way to generate wealth is to identify and anticipate needs, and to create products or render services to meet those needs. Protect, licence and patent your products and services for repeat and perpetual income.

Would you like to start thinking like a millionaire? Change the questions you ask. Begin to ask possibility and necessity questions and within a short time you change your life.

46. A.S.K.: Attitude, Skills and Knowledge

What is the quality of your attitude, skills and knowledge? Sharpen your tools. Be alert. Enhance your ideas with productive right attitude, skills and knowledge. Engage in a never-ending constant improvement, preparation, alertness and anticipation for change and innovation.

Challenge your limiting beliefs and start replacing them with empowering ones, and instantly you change your life. The questions you ask, your attitude and beliefs are either the blocks or the leverage for abundance in your life.

You are living a life of poverty and not living a life of abundance neither because you lack money, capital, power, education nor because you have poor social and economic background and status but mainly if not solely because you lack empowering beliefs, lack expanding right attitude, and you lack income and wealth generating fertile ideas.

Begin to cultivate positive attitude, to learn new skills and to acquire necessary knowledge to choose, create and grow wealth and abundance for yourself and others.

47. The three key leverages for wealth and abundance

Three things are important to change an idea into the money tree. Yes, it is important to engage yourself in what you love. That is an excellent starting point. I would like to emphasise, however, that to turn your labour of love into income and wealth generating venture requires leverages of **time, money and experience**.

You can live a comfortable illusionary life of security by selling your time for money but over the ages it has been proven that there is a limit to how much you can earn in exchange for your 24/7 hours of labour for money.

Indeed the vivid way to view it is to compare how much load you can carry on your head or back in relation to using the leverage of a wheel barrow, trucks, trains, ships and aeroplane.

To build wealth you need the leverage of money, time and experience to turbo drive your business.

48. Get on networking or referral marketing

What will give these leverages of time, money and experience? Networking, referral, relationship or permission marketing are for us today in the twenty-first century exactly what printing press, steam engine, the industrial revolution, mechanised farming, and automated mass production were to our ancestors.

There are a lot of them to choose from. Look for a well-managed one that deals in the ultimate consumable that everyone needs and uses everyday and everywhere. You also need to check out their track records, especially their compensation plan, their profitability and growth, their board of management, and their training programmes and support for the new recruits.

A good one should meet the basic three leverages of time (flexible to run on your own convenient time and preferably part-time to start with); little start-up money; and little experience as training and support should be easily accessible to you.

I would like to warn you that it is not a get-rich-quick business. It requires a lot of consistent and persistent effort over a period of time, usually within three to seven years depending on your efforts and attitude and skills.

Those who are teachable often perform better than the clever ones who want to do things their own way.

It is not a lot of money for no effort, but compared with the normal work life of fifty hours a week, fifty weeks a year, for fifty years with no guaranteed pension, there is no doubt that it is well worth every minute of seven years to build up a willable residual income that will keep growing even when you are sleeping, ill or on holiday and when you have retired and stopped working!

49. Use the magic power of dream, desire and purpose

The mystery of dream has fascinated every human generation. What is so intriguing about dreams? What is the link between dream and desire? What is the connection between dream and our purpose in life?

Whether we remember them or not, we all dream several times every night. We all have our dreams and desires. And when we ignore certain desires and dreams, we also have certain feelings of discomfort! I would like to simplify the mystery of dream.

Dreams are common and available in every culture because it is the language of the universe. The universe uses it to communicate our mission and destiny in life because everyone can understand it. It is like the other universal languages of laughter, love and pain.

The lives of successful people demonstrate to us that our dream, purpose, destiny or mission in life is a gift and a blessing. The joy of using our talent or gift is not only in the pleasure of pursuing our dreams but also in the ineffable moment of their completion, achievement and accomplishment.

50. The curse of neglected dreams

The sad news is that when a blessing is ignored it becomes a curse. We feel pain and we become uncomfortable when we ignore the gift of a dream, a mission, a purpose or indeed our destiny! We are restless and bored when we ignore our dreams.

The purpose of a river is to flow. The purpose of the sun is to shine and radiate. Each and every one of us has a purpose to use our endowments to choose, create and grow a joyful life for ourselves and for others.

The desire to meet the ultimate purpose for joy and happiness is encoded in our nature. It is what drives us. They are the basic needs for food, shelter and warmth. They are the psychological needs for love or connection, security and significance and the spiritual needs for self actualisation, contribution and leaving a legacy.

We are only truly alive when we are in the **never-ending process** of pursuing and realising our purpose. On our deathbeds we will not remember how long we stayed in the office, how high our edifices were, and what other things we have acquired or not acquired, we would only either regret neglected dreams or be pleased with leaving the world a better place.

Maybe we can only truly learn how to live when we have learnt how to die! Just for a moment contemplate on the last word of the late Elizabeth Barrett, the wife of

Robert Browning, the famous English poet. The husband asked her how she felt and in just one word before she passed on, she said, 'BEAUTIFUL!'.

The only joy on the relaxed and peaceful face of a dying person is the invaluable satisfaction and pleasant memories of a finished business and a fulfilled dream or purpose! The feeling of mission accomplished!

51. The last hours on the deathbeds!

I once worked in a nursing home and I had the privilege of seeing the last moments of people in the home. Some wished they could turn the clock back to live their dreams and some were totally serene and happy after a good life!

In order to meet our needs we are all endowed with enthusiasm. Enthusiasm is our innate source of energy to pursue and accomplish our destiny: beliefs, needs, desires and purpose. And because it is in the interest of the universe that we are alive and successful with our purpose, each time we make a **decision and a commitment** to pursue our purpose, the universe conspires to help us.

I challenge you to examine your life and to ask yourself the hard question! Hard question leads to easy life. Easy question results in hard life. Face the hard questions. Living a life of abundance requires asking and answering the hard and difficult questions. What would you regret if you were to die tonight?

Resolve to immerse, commit and pursue it with all your endowments. An eighty-year old man was asked, 'what is the point in pursuing a university degree at your age', and his reply was that it was much easier for him to do so than to waste the rest of his life agonising and regretting not doing it. Why not begin right now that you can do something about it?

You owe it a duty to save yourself the saddest moment of unfulfilled and neglected dreams. From my experiences of the last hours with the dying I want to assure you that every effort you put into pursuing your dream in life is worth the joy, peace and serenity of that last breath!

52. Beginner's luck and the victor's test: both would pass!

The universe has an incredibly good sense of humour! When the universe wants to laugh, it grants our self-conceited wishes. Because everything is connected to everything else the universe is only interested in the whole, not the parts. What connects everything is the present. It connects the past with the future. It connects the rich with the poor and it connects the old with the new.

The secret of living a life of abundance is to live in the moment. Live in the moment and you can improve it. And since today is the tomorrow we feared yesterday, living and making the best of the moment is the assured way of a better tomorrow. Courage, persistence and patience are reliable allies in our journey through life. They are effective tools to do the job of living. Always take them with you, wherever you go. They work.

53. The Chinese Bamboo

Living a life of abundance requires a lot of patience. It is like growing a Chinese bamboo. It takes four years to germinate, but when it shoots out you can literally see it growing eighty feet in a few days. Leave your seed in the ground. Step back and let it grow. With good soil, adequate watering, a proper scarecrow, you would soon have a bounteous harvest.

54. How do you grow confidence?

I would like to share with you the moral of that famous and classic book: *The Greatest Salesman in the World* by Og Mandino. Hafid, the hero of the book, had to learn how to deal with the fear of rejection.

Courage, persistence and consistency are important qualities in dealing with the risk and fear of rejection. It took me more than six months to develop enough courage to walk out of my house door to approach people to be my customers.

The secret of it all is that it is a number game. What you lack in skill, you can make up for in numbers. Just knock on more doors. Make more phone calls. Write more letters. Just do more than those who are skilful. Pretty soon you too will become skilful. I told a friend who is a Jehovah's Witness and he also confirmed knocking at the first door is the most difficult step to take!

I went out properly dressed and, with the same spirit with which I walked on coal fire, I shot my chest out to lead me. I had a good smile on my face and as I faced rejections upon rejections I kept on telling myself that each rejection leads me closer to that yes. After about three hours of door-to-door I came up with a solid appointment.

I have built up my confidence because I was totally determined to keep going regardless of the number of rejections. There is always that yes around the corner. I only need to keep going to find it. After every nine nays, there is always a yes! Thanks for being one of the nine. Your nay has drawn me closer to Number Ten!

At the end of the day I decided to keep knocking at least twenty doors each day, three or four days a week, for the next ninety days. The goal is to get one customer per week for the next ten months.

Please always remember that warlords and generals do feel fear not only for themselves but for their troops because of the risk of lives. Feel the fear but do it anyway is the golden rule for dealing with the butterflies of uncertainties. The only certainty I can I assure you is that every success drives away the mirage of fears.

Go out today to face and slay that dragon standing between you and a life of abundance.

55. It is a game of 'do-it-yourself'

No one can help you do it. You and only you can do it for yourself. I manufactured many excuses but I found out that there is no alternative. The ball is in my court. It is up to me to play it the way I want. Remember the ten most powerful two-letter words: if it is to be, it is up to me!

56. Be practical and sentimental, not logical and reasonable!

Successful people are however able to do what they don't want to do because they have a strong emotional or sentimental type of purpose that is neither reasonable nor logical. There is neither motivation nor inspiration in logic. There is neither drive nor courage in logic. Neither is there happiness nor joy in logic. The only place logic has in living the life of abundance is that it is only in meeting the wants and desires of others that yours are met.

Your purpose must be practical not visionary. Needs are logical while wants are sentimental and emotional. Your needs will push you just so far, but when your needs are satisfied, they will stop pushing you. If however your purpose is in terms of wants and desires, then your wants and desires will keep pushing you long after your needs are satisfied and until your wants and desires are fulfilled.

The other significant role of passionate purpose is that when the going gets tough; when it seems all the roads are blocked; when friends and family demand you to be sane, reasonable and realistic; when you have been confronted with obstacles, rejections and frustrations; and in those moments of the dark nights of the Soul, it is only a strong and passionate purpose that will remain the traveller's or the hero's reliable ally and companion.

And what is more important and crucial is that in your adventure in life, you will never succeed beyond the purpose to which you are willing to surrender!

57. Eat that frog first: Do what failures will not like to do!

Many years ago, Albert E. N. Gray, an official of the Prudential Insurance Company of America, found out that the common denominator for success is that successful people do what failures won't do. In his memorable address at the 1940 National Association of Life Underwriters annual convention in Philadelphia, Gray noted that successful people, like failures, don't like to do what failures won't do but they do it because without doing it they would not be able to do what they want to do. More recently Brian Tracy, author and public speaker, refers to doing what you don't like but would stand in your way to success as eating that big frog first.

So what is holding you up from beginning to live a purposeful life of abundance? For me I would do anything to escape tidying up my house. I would do anything to avoid making a business or sale phone call. I would do anything to avoid selling! I am outstanding in manufacturing excuses for not selling: bad weather, being a stranger, being a black man in a predominantly white rural area!

I was creative, constructive and imaginative with excuses. I was never short of excuses. But what is the reality? Could I build any business without customers? Definitely, no!

What options have I got? Do it now! Begin it! Pick up the phone! Get out and make that call! Some will! Some won't!! So what? Next! And as I took the first step to get out of my house I broke the barrier. I broke the shackles and chains of poverty. I broke the bonds of procrastination.

And as I consistently and patiently and tenaciously make and keep my plans, commitment and resolution to keep going, I realised that my fears were unfounded. Walls began to turn to doors; opportunities started sprouting and running my way. I became lucky! You too can be lucky! Success is one percent inspiration and ninety-nine percent perspiration or tenacity to do what failures will not like to do. Start now!

Be successful. Begin to do the things failures don't like to do so that you can accomplish the things you want to accomplish. Allow yourself to be influenced by the desire for pleasing results. Failures are influenced by the desire for pleasing methods and are inclined to be satisfied with such results as can be obtained by doing the things they like to do.

58. S.T.A.R.T.: Self image, Target, Action, Response and Tenacity

I love the START acronym coined by Paul McKenna, author and public speaker. It brings together five key factors of success and living a life of abundance. All successful people have a powerful **self image**.

They believe in themselves, they believe in their

ideas and they have faith in their ability to make a difference and they want to leave the world a better place.

How else could we explain the commitment of the Wrights brothers? How else could we explain the life of Nelson Mandela? How else could we account for the life of Mahatma Ghandi?

Shakespeare has put it well. The lives of great people teach us that we too could make our life sublime. Start now.

Target is another name for goal, purpose, dream or mission. What are you ready to surrender and commit yourself to do? The bigger your purpose the bigger the energy it generates to drive you. Purpose is the leverage, the propeller and the prime mover for all things. Have a definite purpose; commit and resolve to follow your target, and you will be unstoppable.

You may be delayed but you will never be denied!

Action! Action!! Action!!! Five frogs were sitting on a log. One of them thought of jumping into the pool. How many frogs are left on the log? Well if you are a clever thinker, you are right to say there are four. But are there really four left? No, all the five are on the log.

And here is another one for you. Five candles were lit before five saints meditating and contemplating to blow off the candles. They were still for a while. How many candles were blown off? Well, your guess is as good as mine.

Thinking, contemplating, and meditating without action will not move mountains. Get a plan, get into action and, if you like, work and pray God to bless your actions or tie the camel and pray Allah for protection.

Whatever you believe in, I am afraid, you will need to be awake to pursue and realise your dream.

Take massive actions. They yield massive results.

Start now. Do it now.

Response! Life is neutral. The universe is neutral. Disaster is neutral. Calamities and fortunes are events.

All events are neutral. It rains on the righteous and on the '*wrongteous*'! Tsunami, tornado, floods, drought, wars, inflation, persecution and abuse, discrimination and exclusion, and all forms of human and natural events are facts and reality of life.

They only carry the power and value we give them. They are only as significant as the meaning and interpretation we give them. No wonder Shakespeare reflected that there is nothing good or bad only thinking makes it so!

How do you respond to events? How flexible are you? Do you have cherished opinions? Are you for or against events? Do you fight or make an effort to understand events? The quality of your life is a function of your response to events.

Begin to choose, create and grow empowering and enabling response instead of disempowering and entrapping response to events.

Be responsible (response able). Take responsibility (response ability) for your life!

Begin to study events and to learn to understand them. Begin to study the patterns of events and to learn to anticipate and prepare for them.

Patiently learn how to deal with, to cope with, and adapt to events. Be creative, constructive and proactive to events and you will have equipped yourself with one of the greatest secrets of success and the secret of living a joyful and happy life.

Please let me clarify and don't get me wrong. Understanding events is not the same thing as agreeing with them. Anticipating and responding proactively to events is not complacency, bigotry or reactionary. It is simply the Rudyard Kipling's wisdom of changing what you can and accepting what you can not, and the serenity of treating both disaster and triumph indifferently! Take heed and be wise.

Tenacity is the last glue for all the factors. We eat everyday. We sleep everyday. We excrete and recreate everyday. So must we make and keep our commitments everyday.

Consistency and persistence to constant and never-ending improvement in all areas of our lives are nuts and bolts unifying, sustaining and preserving a perpetual life of abundance.

The day we slip and neglect our purpose, miss our target, stop acting and responding positively with tenacity to the neutral events that are facts and reality of life is the day we get into a slump. So, be prepared and alert.

59. B-A.L.E.R.T. Blue print, Act, Learn, Exercise, Relax and Think.

Develop a **blueprint** for your purpose in life and **act** on your blueprint, and be prepared for the unexpected and uninsurable eventualities. Remember the planet earth is a physical world of duality, contradictions and opposites. Be aware of the contradictions. So, plan your life, but be flexible with your plans. Life is what happens to us while we are pursuing our plans. Be alive. Accept, expect and live with the unexpected. They will come and pass, regardless!

Take action but be patient and remain connected with life. Do without doing, see without looking, listen without hearing and pursue your purpose with effortless efforts.

Learn and study to understand events, and at the same time bear in mind that the wisest person is the one who knows and admits ignorance. If you cannot be a bookworm, be a tapeworm.

Exercise your body, mind and spirit.

Relax and have fun and enjoy your life and all things you do. Remember that you came to this world with nothing and you would be lucky to go with linen and coffin and that the world would be here when you are no longer here. Most of the things we consider so important today may not really be that important and urgent in one hundred years' time.

Think and put things in their proper perspective. Look at the big picture and remember that even this event, phase in your life, this trauma, and indeed even yourself would pass!

60. Slow down: The first casualty of speeding was at 4 mph!

You might be familiar with more haste, less speed. Imagine the delay after an accident. But it is in all areas of our life. That extra day could make all the difference in the proof reading of your report or book. Living a life of abundance begins with having all the time to do the things you love to do.

I would like to share this story with you. Do you know that in 1896, Bridget Driscoll, a housewife from Croydon, United Kingdom, became the first pedestrian in the world to be knocked down and killed by a motor vehicle? Do you know that she was killed when she stepped off a London curb straight into the path of a car travelling at 4 mph? Do you know that, four years before the Model T Ford brought motoring to the masses, the British parliament imposed a 20 mph limit on public highways in 1904?

It is important to stop and think and appreciate that with all our fast world and gadgets, the pyramids were constructed, the *Holy Bible* was written, the *Holy Qur'an* was revealed to a prophet who could neither read nor write, and the *Magna Carter*, Shakespeare plays, and the American Constitution were all produced in the pedestrian old days!

I hope you are not thinking that I am nostalgic about

the good old days of outside toilets! No! That is not me at all. I am not. I love and enjoy the power of word processing, and I could not contemplate going back to writing books with typewriter.

What I am on about is that living a life of abundance requires making room to appreciate those little things such as watching the sun setting; realising that the stars are brighter on very dark nights; and appreciating the joy of watching the staggering first steps of a child and the smile and laughter of children without teeth!

61. What if you were a butterfly with a life span of ten days?

Imagine you were a butterfly with a life span of ten days! What would you do to enjoy your ten days and to leave behind the memory of a brilliant summer and a life well-lived?

I don't know what is going on in your life at the moment, but here is an excerpt from an e-mail I received from a friend while writing this booklet:

'Good to hear from you. Bola, I moved . . . to be near my family. We have had a very trying time recently. My son's wife was diagnosed with Breast Cancer one day, her brother was given 2 weeks to live the next day, and her father was diagnosed with incurable cancer the following day! Since then, Jane (not her real name) has had her operation to have her breast removed and reconstructed – is still extremely poorly in hospital; her brother died; and her father is now dying. It's had a major impact on all the family, and I have been supporting my son, as much as possible. As you can imagine when tragedy strikes you don't have time to think of all the other incidental issues'.

I would like you to note that living a life of abundance means putting things in perspective. Be aware of the incidentals and do not apportion too much significance to the incidentals. Both the incidentals and the significant events such as the experiences of my friend's family will all pass.

62. Seven significant books on living a life of abundance

There are occasions when we are faced with hard choices. This is one of such occasions for me. I have read over three thousand books on personal development and here I am recommending seven for your use. I would like you to use them as the starting point for what maybe a life-long research. My rationale for the selection is that each of the book was a breakaway, a breakthrough, a pioneer for the generation of other authors. And here is my verdict:

1. *Pollyanna*, Eleanor H. Porter (1913). This is as far as I can tell the first book and definitely a classic one to promote the game of positive mental attitude from an innocent child's point of view;
2. *The Science of Getting Rich*, Wallace D. Wattles (1910). A pioneer book on the principles of doing the right thing, in the right way, and at the right time. This booklet is available free on the www.science-ofgettingrich.net;
3. *The Richest Man in Babylon*, George Clason, (1926). Clason using fable came up with the seven principles for amassing wealth. Use the seven principles and you will never be in want, ignore any of them and you may always be poor and miserable;

4. *Think and Grow Rich*, Napoleon Hill (1937). Not only is this a classic book on the principles of success but the author is the first person to actually put across the message that you don't succeed by studying failures, and you don't become healthy by studying diseases. You succeed by studying success. It is a report of over twenty years of the study of success and successful people. The ideas in the book are proven and tested and will remain valuable for many generations to come;

5. *The greatest Salesman in the World (and Part II End of the Story)*, Og Mandino (1967, 1975).These two books are a must for anyone who wants to live a life of abundance. The secret of the books is not the title of selling and being successful in sales but rather the subtle messages of giving, of compassion, of consistency and persistence, of courage, of charity and love, of gratitude and recognition of human invaluable endowments of choice and attitude;

6. *Rich Dad, Poor Dad: What the Rich Teach Their Kids About Money the Poor and Middle Class Do Not* by Robert Kiyosaki (1997; Part II *Cash Flow Quadrant* 1998; and Part III *Rich Dad's Guide to Investing* 1999). Kiyosaki humorously throws light on the road to financial success and freedom; and

7. *The 8th Habit: From Effectiveness to Greatness*, Stephen Covey (2004). You will find the principles in different shapes and forms from other writers but they are best put together by Professor Covey.

As I said at the beginning I have selected these books as a starter for you in the constant and never-ending process of developing a life of abundance.

63. Seven spiritual laws of living a life of abundance

This is another challenge. There are many universal laws. They are immutable and when you break them you pay for them regardless of your ignorance of them. What I am going to do here is to bet on my confidence that once you obey the following you will have started to learn about the rest. The laws are:

1. **The law of awareness, faith, belief and values:** We are what we believe and we can only rise to the limit of our faith and beliefs. Be aware of your beliefs, values and thoughts and consciously monitor them. Thoughts are things. The law is also expressed as the law of expectation;

2. **The law of intention or purpose:** We are driven in life by our purpose or intention. Have a big purpose and you will surmount any obstacle. Have a little purpose and you will achieve little. Raise your standard and purpose and you will dramatically change your life. You will always be bored, restless and uncomfortable when you operate lower than your mission, purpose or dream in life;

3. **The law of cause and effect:** Some call this the law of karma or the law of the farm or the law of boomerang, or the law of action and reaction. You reap what you sow, so be the cause and not the effect; be proactive and not reactive. We come across this law in our everyday communications and dealings with life. We shout to the mountain, the mountain shouts back; we are angry with life and life is angry with us! We laugh with life and life laughs back!

4. **The law of attitude:** Life is one percent what happens to us, and ninety-nine percent how we react to what happens. The value and the meaning

we add to neutral events are more important than the events in themselves. Change your perception and association to events and you change the game. By all means enjoy the game and take away your attachment to the outcome and you will be blessed with the multiple returns of one of the greatest secrets of living a life of abundance;

5. **The law of action and response:** Life is about action and responsibility. Nothing happens until we make them happen. How do we respond to our feelings? Our motions determine our emotions. Change your motion, take action and keep moving and you will have a new lease of life;

6. **The law of balance and harmony:** Do the right thing at the right time and in the right way. It is also the law of economy. The right action for the desired result. The right tool for the job. And remember to sharpen the tools of patience, attitude, courage, consistency and persistence; and

7. **The law of love:** This is the most important of all the laws. It is the glue that unites all the other laws. Do all things with love . . . love for yourself, love for all things, love for others, and love for the entire universe.

64. The seven most important words: What do you think?

By now you will have given up on my sanity. But if you have come this far you are probably as mad as I am. So what are the seven most important words?

1. No;
2. We;
3. Our;
4. Us;

5. Mine;
6. They; and
7. I.

The first we are all afraid of because it stands for rejection. We are also reluctant to use it because we want to please others. Hence we overcommit, overload and over-burden ourselves. The rest we use to either connect with, or to separate ourselves from, others.

Living a life of abundance is about understanding, empathy and connection with the universe! The result is joy, happiness, total freedom, wealth and good health. The reverse is equally true. Separation, conflicts and hatred result in misery, bondage, poverty, war and disease!

65. The seven companions for a life of abundance

How could I leave you without some comfort and good news? In my search for the secrets of the successful people who live an enviable life of abundance, I found out that they have seven common companions among others:

1. They are all happy in their own skin and company. They have an excellent self image and they are their own best friends. They love themselves and they feel they are enough as individuals;
2. They are all connected with others and most of them have an excellent family relationship; and the few who are single, widowed or divorced give love and express love with pets and to others in their own way. They all have their individuality and yet relate with others in harmony and with compassion;

3. They all have faith and belief in the goodness of others and they have trust in themselves and in others. Most of them belief in a higher force, and most of them express the force as Universal Intelligence, God, Allah, Chineke, Olodumare, and other names referring to a supreme being;
4. They all have passion for one hobby or sport;
5. They all have a coach, mentor or a role model;
6. They all enjoy travelling and meeting people outside their culture; and
7. They have all created and benefited from companies of masterminds, biographies, good literature and books, and oral stories, and from the wisdom of ages.

66. Embrace these seven habits of successful people

1. Definiteness of purpose;
2. Personal initiative;
3. Controlled enthusiasm;
4. Self-discipline;
5. Going the extra mile;
6. Constructive and creative thinking; and
7. Constant and never-ending improvement and sharpening your tools.

67. Conclusion

I want to thank you again and to say the process of transforming our lives and living a life of abundance requires that we become gardeners and farmers who choose, create and grow a joyful life.

Identify your purpose through a process of identifying what you love and you are connected with.

Look for a market or people ready to buy your interest and hobby.

Dedicate yourself to the labour of love in a field that gives you the opportunity to experience joy, to express your higher self, and to truly connect with your real self and others.

These sixty seven principles, precepts and tips are indeed the secrets, science and systems of living a life of abundance. Learn them. Plug into them and say good bye to poverty.

Please let me know how you are doing. And until we meet again, May the Blessings Be.

Joyfully yours with love,

Bola Dauda
Burscough, December 2005.

The End and the Beginning of Practising and Passing on the Message!

For more information about our programmes please contact:

The Director of Programmes
Freepost RLXA-BZTZ-XXKC Robin Books Limited
3 The Boundary Lane, BURSCOUGH Lancashire L40 5XT
United Kingdom
Coaching website: www.360degreelifecoaching.com
www.360degreelifecoaching.co.uk
E-mail: info@robinbooks.co.uk
Shop online: www.robinbooks.co.uk

Subscribe to the
360° Lifestyle FREE MONTHLY NEWSLETTER!
Here's how. (It's easy!) Just send a blank email to
lifestyle@360degreelifecoaching.com
OR
Go to www.360degreelifecoaching.com
And click on the "NEWSLETTER." link, fill in the form,
and hit "send." And of course . . . tell a friend!

Have you downloaded *Living a Life of Abundance* on the
internet and would like extra copies of it or extra copies of
any of our series to give to loved ones, friends, team
members, prospects and clients?

PAPERBACK QUANTITY DISCOUNT SCHEDULE

Single copies..........US$10.00/UK£5.00 each
10-99 booklets..........US$9.00/UK£4.50 each
100-499 booklets..........US$8.00/UK£4.00 each
500-999 booklets..........US$7.00/UK£3.50 each
Over 1000 copies..........US$6.00/UK£3.00 each

(All UK Orders: £2.50 for up to nine copies and
Free P&P delivery for 10 or more copies.
E.E.C. & other Overseas: 25% of order value).

Company/Group/Charity personalisation is available.

For fast, easy ordering simply call
0800 45 85 397 (in the UK) or
+44 1704 896 277 (outside the UK)
Or visit us at
www.360degreelifecoaching.com

About the author

Dr Bola Dauda is an honorary fellow of the University of Leicester and a life member of The Coaching Academy, United Kingdom. He is a business growth and life coach with passion and speciality in easy, simple and practical way to choose, create and grow a joyful life.

His simple techniques have helped many people to build a new lifestyle of balance and harmony, to readjust their values and beliefs, and to recharge their energy and motivation to pursue their goals and purpose.

Although he is shy to admit speciality, he is definitely at his best in supporting people to write books, academic dissertations and theses, and business reports.

His first book, *The Will to Succeed*, Macmillan, 1981, sold over 100,000 copies. He lives in Great Britain and after successful careers in the civil service and academia; he is now a full-time writer, life coach and public speaker.

Dr Dauda's writings have been universally acclaimed as refreshing, inspiring, uplifting, truthful, down-to-earth and honest.

Contact
e-mail: bola@360degrelifecoaching.com
tel: 0800 4585397 (UK only)
    +44 1704 896 277